HEIRS AND HERITAGE

WALKING IN YOUR PURCHASED INHERITANCE IN JESUS CHRIST

MIGUEL A. SANCHEZ

FOREWORD BY FEMI ADUN

CONTENTS

Acknowledgement | 05

Foreword | 07

Preface | 11

Chapter 1
PRAYING TO SEE | 15

Chapter 2
BLESSED IN CHRIST | 21

Chapter 3
CHOSEN IN CHRIST | 25

Chapter 4
REDEEMED IN CHRIST | 31

Chapter 5
COMPLETE IN CHRIST | 35

Chapter 6
HEALED IN CHRIST | 39

Chapter 7
VICTORY IN CHRIST | 45

Chapter 8
OUR POSITION IN CHRIST | 51

Declaration | 55

ACKNOWLEDGEMENTS

First, I want to thank my Lord Jesus for everything He has done for me, and for what He will continue doing through me for His glory.

I want to thank my wife Gina L. Sanchez for co-laboring in helping me to write this book. Just like the prophetic word that was given to us. Utilizing her writing skills to make me sound good. I love you!

I would like to thank Apostle Femi Adun for being used by God while texting back and forth about other things. Then suddenly, your text changed when you asked me on August 14, 2018, "Bro, when are you going to write your book?" You had no idea about what was in my heart for many years, concerning me writing books. You encouraged me and became the pathway to bring this to a reality.

Lastly, I would like to thank Pastor Joseph Samuel also for confirming that the Lord wanted me to write this book with a prophetic word on Sept 8, 2019, which caused me to say "I really need to get this done now."

A big thank you to Fire At The Altar family for supporting this work. God is doing mighty things through this ministry!

FOREWORD

Often times as believers we talk about who we are in Christ which I consider as the operating system of the new testament Christian. As believers we cannot afford to navigate our Christian life without a deep-seated knowledge and understanding of our identity in Christ as this is what gives us the innate ability to function as sons and daughters of God outwardly. However, another powerful biblical truth every believer must have a revelation of is not just who we are in Christ but also what we have in Christ; our inheritance through His shed blood on Calvary's cross.

According to Romans 8:17 every believer is referred to as heirs of God, which means through Christ you and I are now children of God with paternal rights to His inheritance. It means we are no longer outsiders or slaves; through Christ we became the heritage of the Lord. Heritage is what gives right of claim to your descendants' inheritance. Now that your heritage is in Christ, God wants you to take advantage of all the blessings He secured for you and me in Jesus Christ.

A lack of this knowledge or understanding results into a slave mentality, which has led to many believers begging for what is already theirs as heirs of God. I believe this is what the Apostle Paul was referring to when he wrote Galatians 4:1 *"Now I say that the heir, as long as he is a child, does not differ at all from a slave, though he is master of all"*. When a believer is without the knowledge of what he or she has in Christ, such a believer is not any different from a child with no knowledge of the kind of family he or she has been born into or privileges available to him or her as an heir of that family.

Just like most kids growing up, I grew fond of the fictional character from the movie Tarzan. Tarzan the only human in the jungle grew up with other jungle animals and this was the only family he knew and had. After many years, Tarzan met his first human and that revelation changed everything for him because he suddenly realized there was more to who he was and what he could have. Likewise, there is more for every child of God in and beyond the physical; a life full of glorious inheritance available through Jesus Christ. But it is only in the revelation of who we are and what we have in Christ that unlocks it.

I am very impressed with what Pastor Miguel has done with this book; in the sense that he has carefully articulated through scriptures not only who we are but more essentially what we have in Christ. His passion for every child of God to experience the supernatural life in Christ is undeniably revealed through every sentence. In order to inspire you, his reader to go after your inheritance and live an abundant life in Christ. This book "Heirs and Heritage" is a timely book especially at a time when the entire world is undergoing a shift in the social, political and economic structure which has led to the circulation of fear of social well-being and economic stability. You will discover through the revelation in this book that there is no need to live in fear as your inheritance in Christ covers every area of the believer's life here on earth as well as assures you of your heavenly inheritance.

I highly commend this book, like I do regarding the author himself; a friend turn brother in Christ. Thank you, Pastor Miguel, for providing the body of Christ with this timeless truth in a timely season for our spiritual growth and personal edification. I have no doubt that this book will change the lives of thousands of believers around the world and I pray it will bring millions of lost souls to the saving grace of our lord Jesus Christ, Amen.

Apostle Femi Adun
President, *Eagle World Outreach*

PREFACE

What is our inheritance in Jesus Christ? Well, the definition of the word inheritance is: A heritage, a gift from God or the portion that God has assigned. A thing, a possession or a property that is inherited or willed to you as the beneficiary, after a family member or a friend passes away. With all of this being said, we are the beneficiaries and the rightful heirs to everything that Jesus Christ has passed on to us. We are children of God the Father and joint heirs with Christ Jesus (Romans 8:16 & 17).

Being an heir means that you are the next in line to receive what is yours based on your birth right. For example, if you are the first-born son of a king, then you automatically become heir to the throne and will eventually become the next king. Therefore, once we receive Jesus as our Lord, Savior and King over our lives, we automatically become the next in line to receive what is rightfully ours in Him.

For when we were born again, we became qualified due to our spiritual birth as sons and daughters of God to inherit what is rightfully ours in the Lord Jesus Christ.

> ***Ephesians 1:1***
> ***In Him also we have obtained an inheritance, being predestined according to the purpose of Him who works all things according to the counsel of His will.***

This verse shows us that we have received an inheritance in Christ. Some of our inheritance is stored up in heaven, to be enjoyed in the future when Jesus comes back again. There is a part of it that we have already received so we can walk in it now. Such as, the new birth experience, the baptism of the Holy Spirit, the gifts of the Holy Spirit, and the anointing of the Holy Spirit. Keep in mind that there is much more to our inheritance. We will experience a new heaven, a new earth and a new body, with which we will never experience death again. We can enjoy an abundant life here and now like Jesus promised and a glorious life to come.

> ***John 10:10***
> ***The thief does not come except to steal, and to kill, and to destroy. I have come that they may have life, and that they may have it more abundantly.***

I pray that as you read this book, God will begin to reveal to you the hidden treasures and promises that He has predestined for your life. It is essential to know and understand what you already have, and what you are entitled to in Him. My prayer is that this book will help you to identify what is rightfully yours, so you can claim it, walk in it and know who you are in Christ Jesus!

14

PRAYING TO SEE

It is so important for you to know what you have already obtained in Jesus Christ! It is not what you are going to receive, but rather what you already have here and now. In Ephesians chapter 1, we see that the apostle Paul was speaking to the church of Ephesus, and he was praying that the eyes of their understanding would be enlightened. He prayed that the spiritual eyes of the church would be opened. What for? What do you do with your eyes? Do you eat with your eyes? Certainly not! Do you speak with your eyes? No! What purpose do eyes serve? Well, eyes give you the ability to see. Here we see that Paul was not praying for the physical eyes to be opened. Instead, Paul was praying for their spiritual eyes to open. He prayed this so that the church at Ephesus could see what was lawfully theirs in Christ.

Ephesians 1:17 & 18
That the God of our Lord Jesus Christ, the Father of glory, may give to you the spirit of wisdom and

revelation in the knowledge of Him, [18] the eyes of your understanding being enlightened; that you may know what is the hope of His calling, what are the riches of the glory of His inheritance in the saints.

Paul was not speaking of hearing about this only. He was insinuating that you would come to know this first-hand by experiencing it on your own. First-hand knowledge outweighs any information that you are taught, or learn by seeing someone else do. The actual tangible experience that you encounter will trump everything else. For example, you can read about giving birth and you can watch someone give birth. However, until you actually go through the experience of giving birth yourself, it will simply remain as head knowledge without actually ever experiencing it.

Ask yourself this question: Do I want revelation in the knowledge of Jesus?

Ephesians 1:18
That the eyes of your understanding been enlightened.

When your spiritual eyes are enlightened, darkness will go. This will allow you to see clearly. Here is an example of what I mean: When you walk into a dark room, you have difficulty seeing what is around you. However, once you turn on the light, then you will be able to see everything clearly. Things in the room were there already, but you were unable to see it because there was no light. Likewise, God has already given us an inheritance, which we will only be able to see it once our spiritual eyes have been illuminated.

Paul was not speaking about hearing of this. He was speaking about you knowing about this first-hand by experiencing it on your own.

Once you become a believer in Jesus Christ, you are then set apart and are considered to be in right standing before God. Thus, you have become a saint and you now have the right to receive the inheritance that He has for you. Paul said, that you might know the inheritance that's in you. When Jesus died and you received Him as Lord and Savior, the Holy Spirit deposited an inheritance on the inside of you. That means that it is in you already. As you grow in the knowledge of Christ and in His word you will begin to see what exactly has been deposited on the inside of you. When you deposit a check into your bank account, you then have to check online to see that the deposit went through successfully. When the Holy Spirit opens up your spiritual eyes you will be able to see that the deposit went through and it is available for use.

Paul prayed for revelation so you can see not what is outside of you, but rather what is on the inside of you! You need to shift your mind away from seeing yourself from the outside, and begin to see yourself with your spiritual eyes and what you have on the inside of you. Once you are able to capture the revelation of what you have inside of you, then you will begin to live a victorious Christian life.

You will know your inheritance in Christ and the power and authority you have in this life. Satan will no longer be able to take advantage of you. In the book of Hosea it says, "My people perish for a lack of knowledge." Once you have the knowledge of your inheritance, you will not perish in life but rather you will prosper in life.

> ***Hosea 4:6***
> *My people are destroyed for lack of knowledge. Because you have rejected knowledge, I also will reject you from being priest for Me; Because you have forgotten the law of your God, I also will forget your children.*

Everything that you need to live a successful Christian life, God has already placed it on the inside of you. The scripture says "Christ in you the hope of glory." *(Colossians 1:27)* Jesus lives in you through the person of the Holy Spirit, and that is all that you need in this life to live victoriously. Jesus said, "Rivers of living waters shall flow out of you." So where are those rivers of living water? It is inside of you waiting to flow out. Jesus did not say "river". He said "rivers", which is plural meaning more than one. What are these rivers? They are rivers of healing, rivers of deliverance, rivers of the favor, the blessings and the power of God. Amen! How do we walk in those blessings? By seeing what we have in Christ.

> ***2 Corinthians 3:11***
> *For if what is passing away was glorious, what remains is much more glorious.*

In the old covenant they experienced the glory of God, but in this new covenant that we have it is much more glorious. That is because in the old covenant God was with them, but in the new covenant, GOD is in us.

> **2 Corinthians 3:12**
> **Therefore since we have such hope, we use great boldness of speech.**

We are bold in the new covenant due to the blood of Jesus. Boldness means no reservations, so we can go straight to His throne and ask God for anything according to His perfect will.

> **2 Corinthians 3:14**
> **But their minds were blinded. For until this day the same veil remains unlifted in the reading of the Old Testament, because the veil is taken away in Christ.**

Anyone who reads the scriptures without Christ in them has a spiritual veil. That veil is only taken away after you receive Christ Jesus. Once again this veil, or spiritual blindness is taken away only in Christ.

> **2 Corinthians 3:16**
> **Nevertheless when one turns to the Lord, the veil is taken away.**

In verse 14 it states "but their mind was blinded. For until this day the same veil remains not lifted in the reading of the old testament, because the veil is taken away in Christ."

Only in Christ is this veil taken away. If we see a room full of blind people, we will feel compassion for them and begin to wish that they could see. But spiritual blindness is worse than physical blindness. Physical blindness will affect you only in this world, but spiritual blindness will affect you in this world and the world to come. That spiritual veil is removed from the hearts and minds of people when Christ is believed on and received. When people have cataracts in their physical eyes they cannot see clearly, but with modern technology they can now remove cataracts. Once you are born again, your spiritual cataracts are removed so you can begin to see clear. Therefore, when you start reading the scriptures, you can see spiritually and understand spiritually what the word of God says. Thank God because once we were blind, but now we can see. Declare, "I can see in Christ!"

CHAPTER 2

BLESSED IN CHRIST

Ephesians 1:3
Blessed be the God and Father of our Lord Jesus Christ,
who has blessed us with every spiritual blessing in the
heavenly places in Christ.

Take note that Paul often references "in Christ" and "in Him" throughout the scriptures. What does this mean? This means that everything we receive, has to be received in Christ or in Him. This is because God the Father has deposited everything into Jesus Christ. Therefore, once we receive Jesus, we also receive all that he has on the inside of Him. We become rightful partakers of everything that He has for us. A physical illustration would be a when a woman is pregnant and the baby is inside of her, the baby partakes of everything that she eats and drinks. So you being in Christ are partaking of every spiritual blessing that Christ has received from the father.

Ephesians 1:3 declare that we are blessed with every spiritual blessing in the heavenly places in Jesus Christ! Here we can see one of the many benefits of our inheritance. We are already blessed in Christ Jesus! Please understand that this does not mean that we are going to be blessed, but rather it means that we are already blessed. This scripture references that we are already blessed with every spiritual blessing in the heavenly places here and now. How do we get the blessings that we have stored up in heaven down here on earth? We can access those blessings in heaven here on earth through prayer. That is the key to accessing our heavenly blessings. As Jesus prayed, Your Kingdom come, your will be done on earth as it is in heaven. The spiritual blessing of God on us manifests all kinds of blessings. So what we received is "the" blessing, which is greater than "a" specific blessing. You can lose a specific blessing but you cannot lose the blessing, which will bring all blessings to you. As an example, if you were to lose your job, then you would have just lost a specific blessing. However, since you have "the" blessing, then you are empowered to find another job.

Galatians 3:13 & 14
Christ has redeemed us from the curse of the law, having become a curse for us (for it is written, "Cursed is everyone who hangs on a tree"), [14] that the blessing of Abraham might come upon the Gentiles in Christ Jesus, that we might receive the promise of the Spirit through faith.

Here we can see that the blessing of Abraham is released to those who are in Christ. If you are outside of Christ, then you will never experience the blessing of Abraham because it is found only in Christ. Once you are in Christ, your obedience activates the blessing of Abraham. Disobedience will deactivate the blessing from flowing. Obedience activates the blessing to flow. Abraham, Isaac, Jacob, Joseph, David, and Jesus all walked in the blessing of Abraham. Now this blessing has come upon us in Christ. Begin to declare that the blessing of Abraham and all the promises of God are yours.

> ***Corinthians 1:20***
> ***For all the promises of God in Him are Yes, and in Him Amen, to the glory of God through us.***

All of the promises are yes and amen. So every promise you see in the scriptures from Genesis to Revelation, God says YES to every promise in Christ. He is waiting for you to say "amen" to those promises. He is waiting for you to come into agreement with the promises of God. God has promised you something, so just receive it by faith. The promises are received through faith. There are many promises over our lives, but you have to go in and possess the land. God says, "Yes" to the promise! He is simply waiting for you to come in agreement and say amen to that promise.

For all the promises of God are in Christ! You have promises through the written word and you have prophetic promises over your life. You have the rhema promise and the logos promise, which is the written word of God. The rhema word is when God speaks a specific word to you. For instance, God told my wife and I to come to Tampa, FL. Not to Alaska. Tampa was the rhema word for us, but it does not mean that it is the rhema word for everyone else to move to Tampa, FL. There are things that God is going to speak to you and promise you and you alone. Then there will be things that He will tell someone else to do that He won't tell you to do. What I can tell you is that whether it is a written logos promise or a rhema promise, God says yes to that promise! All the promises are yes and amen in Christ! Declare yes and amen in Christ for all of His promises in your life!

CHAPTER 3

CHOSEN IN CHRIST

Ephesians 1:4
Just as He chose us in Him before the foundation of the world, that we should be holy and without blame before Him in love.

We see in this scripture that we have been chosen in Christ before the heavens and the earth were created. He chose you before you chose Him. The reason you and I choose Him, is only because He chose us. He drew you to Himself and you responded to that pull of Love. To think that God chose you before He said let there be light is amazing! If you were ever rejected, rejoice because God has chosen you already. Even with all of your flaws and mistakes in life, you are the chosen in Christ. You were God's choice and God makes no mistakes! Why did He choose you? It is all because of what Christ did on the cross.

Revelations 13:8
And all the people who belong to this world worshiped the beast. They are the ones whose names were not written in the Book of Life that belongs to the Lamb who was slaughtered before the world was made.

This scripture states that the lamb was slaughtered before the world was made. When was Jesus crucified? Was it approximately 2,000 years ago? Or was He killed before that? The answer is, He was killed before 2,000 years ago. You know where? In the mind and in the heart of God, Jesus was crucified before the creation of the world. Wow! What a powerful truth. It happened in the realm of the spirit in eternity where God dwells. Where there is no time and God who knows the end from the beginning, looked into the future before you were born and chose you and said you are mine. At that point before creation happened, God accepted you through Christ. In the realm of time, God created the heavens and the earth. Then on God's timetable, Jesus came physically and died approximately 2,000 years ago, fulfilling the plan that God had in his mind and heart to save us. So He chose you and cleansed you from your sin and separated you to be His child. At that point you were adopted into the family of God.

Ephesians 1:5
Having predestined us to adoption as sons by Jesus Christ to Himself, according to the good pleasure of His will,

This verse tells us that we have been predestined to adoption. We have been adopted in Christ! The difference with Jesus and us is that He is the only begotten Son of God. This means that He has the unique status of being birthed by God. He was born in a miraculous way through the virgin birth. Our natural parents birthed us, but we are adopted by our spiritual father. Jesus will always be the only begotten Son of God, and we will always be the adopted children of God.

Here is some awesome news. Once a family decides to adopt a child, that child then becomes eligible to take part of all of the same privileges that a natural born child would have rights to. Since God the Father adopted us, we now share in the same inheritance that Christ has, and we have a right to use His name and exercise our authority over our circumstances. We have now been named with His name. A good name carries much weight and influence, and the scripture say's Jesus has been given a name, which is above every name, and you have a covenant right as an adopted son to use his name to bring his kingdom power on the scene in your life. So we have been chosen, adopted and accepted in Christ.

> **Ephesians 1:6**
> **To the praise of the glory of His grace, by which He made us accepted in the Beloved.**

Once you receive Him, then He accepts you! God does not reject you. Once you receive Christ, then He is in you and you are in Him. God the Father accepted Christ and He accepts you in him. Outside of Christ you are rejected, only in Christ are you accepted. Why? Because you cannot come to the presence of God the Father except through Christ. It has to be through His blood. Jesus said no one comes to the father except through me. Jesus said, "I am the way", and he also declared I am the door. You cannot get into a house except through the front door. Jesus is the front door.   Once you realize this truth, God's marvellous plans begin to unfold in your life. You begin to see the purpose and plan that God has for you. The plans that God has for you are already pre-planned, you just have to discover them.

> ***Ephesians 2:10***
> ***For we are His workmanship, created in Christ Jesus for good works, which God prepared beforehand that we should walk in them.***

The word workmanship means masterpiece. Have you ever seen an artist draw a wonderful picture? It's like a masterpiece. Well, you are God's masterpiece. He has designed you to be unique, beautiful, with talents and gifts. He has called you and has placed gifts in you that no one else on earth can fulfill but you. Also, no one on earth can be duplicated.

When an artist draws a picture, each picture is unique just as each life is unique. No one can be compared to you, because there is no one else like you. You are God's masterpiece in Christ, and He has created you in Christ for good works. Therefore, the moment you receive Jesus Christ, you begin to discover your call. You will also discover the perfect will of God for your life. God pre-planned your life before he created the world. All that is left for you to do is to discover what that perfect plan is for your life and begin to walk in it. The Holy Spirit will reveal that plan as you walk by faith and seek him. When Abraham obeyed God to leave his homeland, the scripture says he did not know where he was going, but he began to move in the will of God by faith.

> *Hebrews 11:8*
> *By faith Abraham obeyed when he was called to go out to the place, which he would receive as an inheritance. And he went out, not knowing where he was going.*

As He took that step of faith, God continued revealing His perfect will for his life. That is exactly what He does and will continue to do in our lives. Remember that you are God's masterpiece in Christ.

HEIRS AND HERITAGE

CHAPTER 4

REDEEMED IN CHRIST

Ephesians 1:7
In Him we have redemption through His blood, the forgiveness of sins, according to the riches of His grace.

You are not going to become redeemed because you are already redeemed. The word redemption means a release affected by a payment of a ransom. It means to be repurchased, to buy back or to win back what was lost. Adam lost us in the Garden of Eden, but Jesus Christ won us back on the cross of Calvary. God redeemed us before Adam lost us. The bible declares that Jesus was slain before the foundation of the world. The price was paid 2,000 years ago, but when you receive him that sacrifice is made applicable to you. Outside of Christ we are lost, but in Christ we have been found and have been redeemed. We have the forgiveness of sin. How liberating is that? That every sin you have committed has been wiped clean by the blood of Jesus. No need to have any guilt or shame because the blood has covered and destroyed your sin. Never focus on what you have done in your past; just focus on what Jesus did in His past, because His past erases your past. Begin to decree, "I am redeemed in Christ!" Once sin is erased, relationship with God begins, and you who once were far away from God, can now have intimacy with God.

> **_Ephesians 2:13_**
> **_But now in Christ Jesus you who once were far off have been brought near by the blood of Christ._**

According to this scripture, you can now go boldly to the throne of grace through the blood of Jesus. Through His blood we now have access. Think about an example of entering your own home. Of course you will enter boldly into your home because you know that you live there. However, imagine trying to enter the home of an unknown stranger with boldness. You won't be able to do that, right? You can only enter with permission, and the blood of Jesus is our permission to enter the throne of grace. Due to sin, we were once afar off, but because of the blood of Jesus washing our sins away, we have now been brought close to the presence of God. Only in Christ can we come near. Outside of Christ we are far from God. Thank God that we now have access to the most glorious and holiest place in the universe, which is God's throne room.

Hebrews 10:19
Therefore, brethren, having boldness to enter the Holiest by the blood of Jesus.

Since you and I have been shown such mercy and grace we must likewise do the same. We have been forgiven so we must extend the same.

Ephesians 4:32
And be kind to one another, tenderhearted, forgiving one another, even as God in Christ forgave you.

In Christ we have forgiveness of sin. God the Father only forgives you in Christ. Outside of Christ, there is no forgiveness! The price has been paid for everyone to be forgiven, but that forgiveness cannot be received unless you have asked Him to enter into your heart. God has chosen to forgive us of all our sins in Christ. Jesus represents you in heaven, and when you sin all you have to say is "Father in the name of Jesus forgive me" and the Lord will answer that prayer. He will answer because He forgives you in Christ. Christ becomes your representative in heaven as we can see in 1 John 2:1. Say, "I am forgiven in Christ!"

1 John 2:1
My little children, these things I write to you, so that you may not sin. And if anyone sins, we have an Advocate with the Father, Jesus Christ the righteous.

HEIRS AND HERITAGE

CHAPTER 5

COMPLETE IN CHRIST

Colossians 2:10
And you are complete in Him, who is the head of all principality and power.

Apart from Christ, you are incomplete, and no one can make you complete, but Christ. If you are thinking that you want to get married, because you feel that someone else will complete you, think again. A spouse cannot make you complete. If you have children they cannot complete you, only Christ can make you complete! We cannot place that responsibility on another human being who does not have the capacity to fulfill your spiritual life because that is only reserved for Christ.

You are only complete in Christ. And the apostle Paul is the one writing this scripture and the apostle Paul was not married. There are babies that are born with physical defects, and at times, missing body parts; but when you are born again there are no spiritual defects. Your spirit man is made whole and complete in Christ. Everything you need to live a successful life has been deposited on the inside of you. Once you know you are complete in Christ you should no longer have a low self-esteem because you will see you have no lack in Christ. How you see yourself is how people are going to see you. There are people who have spouses, children, money, and good careers and they still feel a void on the inside. Why? That's because the void can only be satisfied in Christ. The scripture states (in Acts 17:28) that in Him we live and move and have our being. Our very being exists because of Him so how can we live separate from Him, when we were made by Him, through Him and for Him.

> ***Ephesians 1:13***
> ***In Him you also trusted, after you heard the word of truth, the gospel of your salvation; in whom also, having believed, you were sealed with the Holy Spirit of promise.***

This verse states that you are sealed with the Holy Spirit. Now you are God's property and anything that belongs to God is His responsibility to take care of. That is why Jesus told us not to worry what you will eat, wear or drink, because your heavenly father knows the things you need. You are His sheep, and He is your Shepherd. The psalmist says, "The Lord is my Shepherd I shall not want." The word "want" means no lack. You will not lack anything when you have the Lord as your shepherd.

> ***Galatians 3:28***
> ***There is neither Jew nor Greek, there is neither slave***

nor free, there is neither male nor female; for you are all one in Christ Jesus.

We see that we are complete, sealed and united in Christ. The spiritual unity that we have in the spirit is supernatural. How God can take people from different nations and cultures and unite us spiritually, is a miracle.

We see that in the spirit it doesn't matter what your gender is or what your race is; none of that matters in the spirit. If you are casting out a devil, it doesn't matter if you're male or female. In the realm of the Spirit, demons only understand authority. It has nothing to do with "only a man can cast devils out". Women can cast devils out too, because it has to do with authority in the spirit. When you were born again, your spirit was recreated in Christ, and you became a new creation in Christ. When I was first saved, I received a new spirit; however, my physical genes did not change. In the spirit it doesn't matter what race, nationality or sex you are. The only thing that matters is that we are a new creation in Christ.

We see that God the Father in Christ has brought forth unity. Where there is neither male nor female, Jew nor Greek, meaning it doesn't matter what you are in the natural, it only matters what you are in the spirit. You could have been racist before being saved but when you were born-again, Christ changed your heart. Hence, you brought racism to the cross and you crucified it. It does not matter if it is a white church or a black church or a Spanish church, it is one church in Christ because in Christ there is unity. It does not matter what color you are. It does not matter where you were physically born, what matters is that you are born-again. Halleluiah! There is racism in the body of Christ, which is a sin because Jesus came to bring unity, not division.

It is one church in Christ bought with the blood of Jesus. And if you are a racist, once you are saved and you still carry that racism with you, just bring it to the cross and let that racism be crucified in you. There is not one race better than the other. Every race has strengths and weaknesses, but when we come together in Christ we collect all the strengths and then we give all the weaknesses to Christ. We are UNITED in Christ!

> *Revelation 5:9*
> *And they sang a new song, saying: "You are worthy to take the scroll, And to open its seals; For You were slain, And have redeemed us to God by Your blood Out of every tribe and tongue and people and nation.*

In this scripture we can see that every tribe, every tongue, and every nation was gathered before the presence of God. Praise God! I rebuke racism in the church in Jesus name! Declare that we are one in Christ!

CHAPTER 6

HEALED IN CHRIST

1 Peter 2:24
Who Himself bore our sins in His own body on the tree, that we, having died to sins, might live for righteousness—by whose stripes you were healed.

He himself bore our sins. Where? He bore our sins on His own body. He carried our sins on His body, on the cross, and then says we having died to sins might live for righteousness.

So when you become a Christian, you are to die to your sin, not live to sin. Meaning, you should no longer continue sinning. Or you should no longer continue practicing sin, because now you are righteous in Christ. Here we see two things taken care of in our lives by the sacrifice of Christ. Our sins are forgiven, and our bodies are healed!

The scripture says in verse 24: By His stripes you were healed. Confess, "I am healed!" Let us emphasize on the "ed" in the word healed. What exactly does that mean? It means past tense. That means you are already healed. Halleluiah!

Isaiah 53:4 says, "Surely, he has borne our grief..." the word grief in the Hebrew is koli, which means sicknesses. In Isaiah 53:4, Isaiah is looking to the future and the Holy Spirit is giving him revelation concerning Christ on the cross. He said, "surely" looking at Jesus on the cross. Surely he has borne or carried our koli or our sicknesses. So not only did Jesus carry your sin, He also carried your sickness too. Jesus took your sickness (koli) on the cross. The price has been paid for you to be forgiven, and the price has been paid so you can be healed. Do you like being sick? Nobody likes being sick. Jesus paid the price so you can receive your healing! So He carried our sin and sickness, and by His stripes we are healed.

They whipped Jesus many times on his back; and every stripe represented your healing. Some people only know about the front of the cross, but there is also the back of the cross as well. Isaiah says, "We are healed" which is indicative of looking toward the future. Then Peter writes this after Jesus' death, burial and resurrection (in 1 Peter 2:24) and looks after the cross, looks to the past and says, "you were healed!" You and I look to the present and say, "I am healed!" Halleluiah! You're not sick trying to be healed, you are healed holding on to your healing.

We serve a present God, not a God who once was. We serve

a God who is! He is the "I AM!" The "I AM" is your healer. The "I AM" your deliverer. The "I AM" your provider. It never says, "I was" your provider, but rather it says, "I AM." Thank God that He does not change. We change, but God never changes. He is the same yesterday, today, and forever. If He healed 2,000 years ago, then guess what, He still heals today. If He delivered 2,000 years ago, then guess what, He still delivers today. If He provided 2,000 years ago then He still provides today.

I AM the GOD that heals you! It is not "I was" as if I don't do it anymore because I lost power, or I no longer know how to do it anymore. You must declare over your own life that you are healed in Christ! The price has been paid! You might ask yourself "why do people still get sick? Why aren't they healed?" Ask yourself this question, "why are there still people who aren't saved?" Christ has already paid the price. So why haven't people received it?

Here is a question for you to ask yourself. How do you receive salvation? It is by grace through faith. How do you receive your healing? It is by grace through faith. It is received through faith. Often times Jesus would tell people "your faith has made you well." So do you think that our faith has something to do with it? Jesus never said, "My power has healed you." Rather, he would say, "your faith has healed you." Here is how Jesus would view it; I have the power, but I need your faith to make the connection. The only reason why people are not saved is because they have not received forgiveness of sins. God has already offered His forgiveness, but all people have to do is receive it. With His stripes you have already been healed. Now receive the healing virtue in your physical body, from the top of your head to the bottom of your feet in the Name of the Lord Jesus, Amen! Praise God! Is your faith being stirred up right now?

All these things are only found in Christ. Apart from Christ, there is no salvation. Apart from Christ, there is no healing. It is only found in Christ.

> ***2 Corinthians 5:17***
> ***Therefore, if anyone is in Christ, he is a new creation; old things have passed away; behold, all things have become new.***

Once we received Christ, we then became a new creation. That new creation experience is only found in Christ. Outside of Christ there is no new creation on the inside of you. Once you received Christ the same power that created the heavens and earth, recreated you on the inside. You were given a new spirit, a born again spirit, and the Holy Spirit came to live on the inside of your newly recreated spirit. At that point, you began to experience this newness of life. Christ in you and you in Christ! You are now one with God, and as you renew your mind with the word of God, you will begin to think in agreement with your new spirit man. Then you will live the life that God has intended you to live, which is an eternal life. This not only means to live forever, but to live the God kind of life.

The God kind of life is a quality of life of walking with God and experiencing his peace, joy and blessings.

HEIRS AND HERITAGE

CHAPTER 7
VICTORY IN CHRIST

2 Corinthians 2:14
Now thanks be to God who always leads us in triumph in Christ, and through us diffuses the fragrance of His knowledge in every place.

Here we see that only in Christ is there victory. Outside of Christ, there is only defeat. Once Jesus was raised from the dead, he obtained victory for us. In life you are going to face problems and trials. However, in Christ, you are going to have the victory over your problems. You are going to have the victory over that temptation, over that oppression, over that depression, over that lack, over that sickness, because God always leads you in triumph in Christ. Begin to declare that you always win. God always wins and the devil always loses! Therefore, we stand firm knowing that we have the victory! Christ has already done all of the hard work. Battles will come and it will seem like sometimes you lose the battle, but you have already won the war. God works all things together for the good of those who love Him. Every negative thing that has happened in your life, God will turn it around for the good. No weapon formed against you, will prosper!

> ***Galatians 2:4***
> ***And this occurred because of false brethren secretly brought in (who came in by stealth to spy out our liberty which we have in Christ Jesus, that they might bring us into bondage).***

Here we see that we have liberty in Christ. Apart from Christ there is bondage, but in Christ there is liberty. In the United States of America, we celebrate Independence Day on July 4th. It's a celebration of our country's Independence from the rule of Great Britain. In contrast to the idea of independence, we as believers must not keep with the mind-set of maintaining independence from God, but rather learn to be completely dependent on God. Your true liberty comes from depending and abiding solely on Him. For the scripture says, "who the son sets free, is free indeed." Many people will try to implement self imposed religion with different man made rules and regulations to try to get you to earn your righteousness, but the apostle Paul warn us to stand in the grace of God and not in works. We are saved by grace through faith, not by works through fear. Be free and stay free in Christ's liberty. He said it is finished. Say "I have liberty in Christ!"

Colossians 1:12
Giving thanks to the Father who has qualified us, to be partakers of the inheritance of the saints in the light."

Here we see that God has qualified us. I want to emphasize on the word "qualified". It is past tense, which means that it already happened. He has already qualified you. You might say to yourself, "When I go to church on Sundays, or when I read my bible every single day, then I'll be qualified." No! He has already qualified you in Christ! There's nothing that you can do to be qualified. He is the one that qualifies you! Religion causes you to do things, in order to become qualified. However, in true Christianity, God qualifies you first. Declare, "I am qualified!" You are qualified to be a partaker of the inheritance. God qualifies you to take part of this inheritance, but you have to read the word of God in order to find out what's your inheritance.

It says you take part of this inheritance in the Light. Who is the Light? Jesus is the light. Jesus is the Light of the world! Therefore, in Him we take part of this inheritance. Obedience activates the blessings. When you walk in the light as He is in the light, then you are able to partake of your inheritance. If you walk in obedience, then the blessings are activated in your life. On the other hand, if you chose to walk in darkness, know that the inheritance is there for you to take part in. However, it will not be activated in your life. It can only be accessed in the light. If you are in darkness, or practicing sin, even though you are a believer, you will not be able to take part in the inheritance that Christ paid for you. Obedience activates the blessings that you already have access to, but disobedience deactivates the blessings. We see that we have liberty in Christ and we are qualified in Christ. We also have deliverance in Christ.

Colossians 1:13
He has delivered us from the power of darkness and conveyed us into the kingdom of the Son of His love.

"He has delivered us." Jesus has delivered us from the power of darkness. When we were sinners, we practiced sin and belonged to a kingdom of darkness. Jesus, the light of the world came and took you out of that kingdom of darkness and transferred you into His kingdom. Therefore, now you and I have been delivered from the hands of Satan, and now we are in the hands of Jesus. The kingdom we now walk in is a kingdom of light, it's a kingdom of power, a kingdom of joy, a kingdom of peace, and a kingdom of blessing, as long as you walk in the light you will experience the glory of the kingdom. When we were in darkness, we experienced darkness. However, when you come to light you experience the kingdom of light.

We are in the world but not of the world! There are two kingdoms on the earth, the kingdom of darkness and the kingdom of light. As sons and daughters of God, we belong to the kingdom of light. For that reason, we will experience everything that the kingdom of light has to offer. When

Israel was in Egypt, God sent the 9th plague, which was darkness over the land. The good news is that the children of Israel had light in Goshen. They were in the region called Goshen and there was light there. The electric company turned off the lights everywhere else except in Goshen. That is because God was Israel's electric company. So while the Egyptians experienced deep darkness, the scripture states (in Exodus 10:21) that it was a darkness that can be felt. Can you imagine how thick that darkness must have been? That's how it was in Egypt. But in Goshen they did not experience a power outage. The difference between the two kingdoms is apparent, because one kingdom experienced light during a time of darkness, and the kingdom of darkness did not have the light that God's people were experiencing. Begin to thank the Father for delivering you from the kingdom of darkness and bringing you into the kingdom of light in Christ.

50

CHAPTER 8

OUR POSITION IN CHRIST

Ephesians 2:6
And raised us up together, and made us sit together in the heavenly places in Christ Jesus

Jesus died, rose again from the dead, ascended and was seated at the right hand of God. We also experienced this spiritually at the same time he experienced death, resurrection, and ascension and now He is in the seated position. This verse means that you have a position of authority. Jesus has been raised far above all principalities and powers, and guess what? You too! God the father and God the son are seated in heavenly places, and so are you. God is the one that has positioned you; therefore, no one will be able to dethrone you. Having this current position, gives you authority and power over all the power of the enemy. In Christ you have authority and power. Outside of Christ, you have no authority or power.

Luke 10:19
Behold, I give you the authority to trample on serpents and scorpions, and over all the power of the enemy, and nothing shall by any means hurt you.

Declare that you have authority in Christ Jesus.

2 Corinthians 5:21
For He made Him who knew no sin to be sin for us, that we might become the righteousness of God in Christ.

Confess, "I am righteous in Christ!" Apart from Christ there is no righteousness! In Christ you have been made righteous. Jesus on the cross is made sin and then we are made righteous when we receive Him. There was a covenant exchange. Jesus says 'Give me all your sin; your lying, your cheating, your stealing, your fornication, your adulteries, "I'll take your sin, you take my righteousness!" When you receive Christ you become just as righteous as Christ is. There is no such thing as two different types of righteousness. It is the same righteousness, which is the righteousness of God. Begin to declare, "I am already righteous!" You must stop thinking like "oh after I give money away, after I go give food to the poor, after I do this and do that, then I am going to become righteous." No, it does not work that way!

"You are already righteous!" You are the righteous in God, doing righteous acts! However, you do not do righteous acts to get righteous, You do righteous acts because you are already righteous. That righteousness is only found in Christ. Apart from Christ you are not righteous, but in Christ you are the righteousness of God. Declare that you are righteous in Christ!

Revelation 1:6
And has made us kings and priests to His God and Father, to Him be glory and dominion forever and ever. Amen!

Say, "I am a king and a priest!" The bible says, that He has made us kings and priests. So we are made kings and priests. Therefore, you are not going to become a king, you already are a king. You are not going to become a priest, you already are a priest. A king is to rule, and a priest is to serve! We have two offices. Say, "I am a king and a priest!" so if you are a king, then you need to begin to think like a king. You need to start speaking like a king, and walking like a king. You are a King! You have dominion in Christ! You are to rule your sphere of domain. You are to rule and reign in Christ. As a priest, you are to perform your priestly duties, which is to minister unto God first and then minister to the people.

1 Peter 2:9
But you are a chosen generation, a royal priesthood, a holy nation, His own special people, that you may proclaim the praises of Him who called you out of darkness into His marvelous light.

Royal means that you have a kingly status. Wow! You are not just a worm or mat that the devil can just walk all over. You have mighty authority and power. You are God's chosen and anointed child. So begin walking and living like the king and priest that you are in Christ Jesus!

DECLARATION

Your confession is your possession! What you declare and decree over your own life will come to pass. No one has more influence over your life, than what you declare out of your own mouth. Here are decrees, declarations and confessions for you to profess over your life in accordance with the word of God.

Psalm 2:7
I will declare the decree: The LORD has said to Me, 'You are My Son, Today I have begotten You.

Job 22:28
You will also declare a thing, And it will be established for you; So light will shine on your ways.

1) I am already blessed with every spiritual blessing in the heavenly places in Christ!

2) I have the blessing of Abraham over my life, and whatever I do prospers.

3) I believe that all of God's promises are yes and amen in my life.

4) I was chosen in Christ before the world was created.

5) I am God's adopted child, and I have the same privileges as Jesus.

6) I am accepted by God.

7) I am redeemed in Christ.

8) I have been brought near to God through the blood of Jesus.

9) I am forgiven in Christ.

10) I have an inheritance in Christ, which includes blessings in this life and in the one to come.

11) I am God's masterpiece in Christ. There is no one on earth like me.

12) I am fully complete in Christ. I have no defects in my spirit man.

13) I have been united with Jesus and every believer worldwide.

14) I have been sealed with the Holy Spirit. I am God's property.

15) I have clarity of sight in Christ. I can see the purpose of God in my life.

16) I am healed in Christ. Jesus took my sin and disease on the cross.

17) I am a new creation in Christ. The blood of Jesus has erased my past.

18) I triumph over every circumstance in life through Christ.

19) I am qualified in Christ, and can partake in all his blessings.

20) I am delivered from the power of darkness. I now live in light.

21) I have liberty in Christ, and I will never be in bondage again.

22) I am seated in heavenly places. I have authority over demons.

23) I am righteous in Christ, and I am just as righteous as Jesus.

24) I am a king and priest. A king to rule, and a priest to serve.

AUTHOR

Pastor Miguel originates from the Bronx, N.Y., where he met his wife Pastor Gina. They began dating in 1994 and later married in 2000. They were blessed with two children, Seth and Seanna.

Pastor Miguel was saved during his teenage years, and due to his father's death it caused him to draw closer to God. On Jan 4, 1998, he was baptized with the Holy Spirit at home in his bedroom. God then led him and his wife to a church named Mission United International in August of 1999, where he would go on to serve in that ministry and co-pastor for the next 12 years. God spoke through a prophetic word to Pastors Miguel and Gina, to leave New York and move to Tampa, FL. That prophetic word confirmed that they were to begin the ministry of Fire At The Altar. Pastors Miguel and Gina launched Fire At The Altar on September 7, 2014, where they are currently pastoring.

Pastor Miguel also travels internationally as an evangelist. He preaches the gospel of Jesus Christ with an undeniable anointing of God. Many lives have been touched through his evangelistic work. As God continues to open up the doors to the nations, Pastor Miguel will continue to say "Here I am Lord, send me!"

Contact Information

Fire_At_The_Altar

Fire At The Altar Ministry

FireAtTheAltar@Yahoo.Com

Fire At The Altar